PRAISE FOR SURVIVING THE HOLIDAYS WITHOUT YOU

"Gary has created a powerful, life-changing resource. If you've lost a loved one or are reaching out to those who are grieving, this book should be the very next thing you read. The valuable content and the practical tips and suggestions will equip you to not only survive the holidays but grow and heal."

–Athena Dean-Holt, Publisher, Redemption Press, Radio Personality, Always Faithful Radio

"When it comes to grief, Gary is sincerely empathetic. His writing is personal, compassionate, and very practical. I know that this book will help many during the holidays."

–Kyle J. Incardona, Managing Partner, Hillier Funeral, Cremation & Bereavement Specialists

"*Reading this book was like listening to a friend giving gentle advice - tips the author learned from his own walk through grief. The title focuses on the holidays, but the tactics ring true for any time of year. I recommend this book with no hesitation and have already shared several copies with friends facing grief from various causes.*"

–Kelli Reynolds, Mays Business School, Texas A&M University

"*Anyone who has experienced grief probably would agree that "surviving" the holiday season is a true sentiment. This book is a practical and easy read for those additional challenges and emotions during the holidays, but really for any day without your loved one. Gary writes from the heart.*"

–Bridgette Shockey, Licensed Clinical Social Worker

"*As a hospice professional myself facing unbearable loss, this book moved my heart into a positive place of healing. I was dreading this holiday season but made a promise to drudge through and make memories for my family regardless of my emotional state. This book fell into my lap,* and now I feel empowered and ready to face this holiday season triumphant. I will be sharing this book with all the hospice team members I work with. What a great read. Thank you."

–Nikki Batten, Hospice Professional

"In this world we live in we expect answers for everything to be at our fingertips immediately. However, there is no search engine that can explain to you how to stop hurting. No website that can replace love that's been lost. Gary provides a beacon of hope. If you are hurting, empty, brokenhearted or the thought of this holiday season leaves dread in your heart because it will only remind you of what has been lost, please, please buy this book and take the time to really sit down with it. I highly doubt you will start and end in the same place."

–Rebecca Brooks, Licensed Clinical Social Worker

SURVIVING
THE HOLIDAYS
WITHOUT

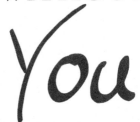

NAVIGATING GRIEF
DURING SPECIAL SEASONS

Thank you for purchasing *Surviving the Holidays Without You.*

These pages are designed as a grief survival kit for special days and seasons.

Please don't read this book just once.

Pick it up again before the next holiday or special time. Come to it again and again.

Each time you will be at a different place.

You'll see your progress. You'll be encouraged. And you'll find your hope has grown.

And please accept this gift. Download your free, printable PDF:

8 Tips for Handling Holiday Grief

https://www.garyroe.com/holiday-grief/

OTHER BOOKS BY GARY ROE

Comfort for Grieving Hearts: Hope and Encouragement for Times of Loss

Teen Grief: Caring for the Grieving Teenage Hearts (Winner, 2018 Book Excellence Award)

Shattered: Surviving the Loss of a Child (2017 Best Book Awards Finalist)

Please Be Patient, I'm Grieving (2016 Best Book Awards Finalist)

Heartbroken: Healing from the Loss of a Spouse (2015 Best Book Awards Finalist, National Indie Excellence Award Finalist)

Co-Authored with Cecil Murphey

Not Quite Healed (Finalist, Lime Award for Excellence in Non-Fiction)

Saying Goodbye: Facing the Loss of a Loved One

DEDICATION

I would like to dedicate this book to my dad, E. L. Roe, and to all the hospice patients and families I've had the honor to serve over the years. I continue to learn from you every day.

ACKNOWLEDGMENTS

Special thanks to Athena Dean of *Always Faithful Radio* for suggesting this project and for all her help in editing and publishing. I couldn't have done this without you, Athena!

Thanks to Don and Sue Wills, David, Kathy, Kay, and Charles who have been so instrumental in my life. You are truly amazing, remarkable people. I'm so honored to be part of your family.

Thanks also to Dr. Craig Borchardt and Johnnie Dominguez for being fantastic men to work under. Thank you for encouraging my writing and supporting me in endeavors that are outside what is typical for a hospice chaplain.

TABLE OF CONTENTS

INTRODUCTION

"What in the world am I going to do about the holidays? There's so much to do, and I have so little energy. My heart is broken. How am I going to survive this?"
Marsha, who lost her husband

"Christmas is coming. What am I supposed to do? She did almost all of it before. I feel so lost. I just want to run and hide."
Stephen, who lost his wife

"I feel lost. It's like I don't know who I am now. I can't even stand looking at family photos."
Jennifer, who lost her daughter

L OSING A LOVED ONE IS painful. Life will never be the same. How could it be?

And if this wasn't hard enough, the holidays are bearing down upon you. What in the world are you supposed to do?

You need a *grief survival kit designed for the holidays.* That's why I wrote this book.

As a hospice chaplain, I've had the honor of walking with thousands of hurting people through deep, dark valleys of grief. I've listened to and observed them on this rocky and emotionally power-packed journey. From my personal grief experiences and theirs, I've gathered some tools that can help you not only survive the holidays, but heal and grow through them.

Here are some *grief truths and tools* that will give you a quick road map of where we're going:

- Holidays are hard. Period.
- This year's holidays will be different, but they can still be good.
- Alone time is good. Isolation is dangerous.
- For the holidays to go well, you must take your heart seriously.
- You get to choose what you do, when, and with whom.

- You'll need compassionate and safe companions for this journey.
- You're not leaving your loved one behind, but moving on *with* them in a new way.
- Don't let the holidays use you. Use the holidays to grieve well and love others.

I believe in you. You can do it.
Take a deep breath. Here we go.

I work as a hospice chaplain and bereavement specialist. I am not a Licensed Professional Counselor and none of my content is meant to diagnose or treat any disease or disorder.

WHY HOLIDAYS ARE HARD

"She's gone now. She was the holiday
queen. Everyone is going to expect the usual
spectacular meal and celebration.
I'm so stressed out."
Sherry, who lost her mother

W HY ARE HOLIDAYS SO HARD sometimes?
The answer is simple: expectations.

We have our own expectations — unspoken
plans and desires roaming around in our heads
about how things should be. Our expectations
often come from the good experiences and
fond memories of the past. We have near
perfect moments back there when all seemed
right with us and the world. It's only natural
to want to recreate that again.

But things never quite work out the way
we expect, do they?

It's been said that *most disappointment in*

life comes from unmet expectations. If enough of our hopes are dashed, over time the wounds of our heart begin to take over. In order to protect ourselves from further pain, we stop expecting the good. We assume things will be difficult, and we prepare to not get what we need and want.

And of course, everyone around us has their own set of unspoken plans and dreams. Our expectations often bump into theirs. Friction occurs and the results aren't always pretty.

In addition, we're continually bombarded by the media-advertising circus whose goal is to redefine and shape our expectations to include their products. This item will make you feel better. That new device will ease your pain. This product will help you forget your losses for a little while. Don't you want to be like the flawlessly attractive and happy people in our commercial?

Our hearts yearn for a better, less challenging world.

Most of us want holidays to be special, fun, and happy. Mixed into that is our desire to please others and make the day special for them. Expectations are swirling around us on all sides.

Talk about stress! It's a wonder anyone survives.

On top of all this, *holidays automatically remind us of those we've lost.*

One Sunday afternoon when I was fifteen, my dad had a massive heart attack and collapsed right in front of me. They managed to resuscitate him at the hospital, but he never regained consciousness. For a week I sat by his bed in the Cardiac Care Unit and talked about anything and everything that came into my mind. The only other sound in the room was the constant hum of the ventilator. I knew he wasn't going to make it.

Since there was no evidence of any brain activity, the doctors finally asked for permission to turn off the machines. My brother was quite a bit older. He nodded. I nodded. I knew dad would never want to live this way. He died several hours later.

I had been living with my dad at the time, just the two of us. It wasn't a perfect relationship (hey, I was a teenager), but I loved him. I have such powerful and fond memories of us together. When he died, I felt lost. He had been my home.

A terrific family I had known for years stepped up and took me in. It turned out my dad had sensed something was going to happen to him and had talked with them about me. Even though they already had four kids, they welcomed me in as one of their own. It was wonderful. They helped me heal.

And then December rolled around. I had always loved the Christmas season and I was having a blast with my new family. But when I woke up Christmas morning, I felt incredibly sad. Though I was happier than I had ever been, my heart was also aching. It was Christmas, and my dad wasn't there. I missed him terribly.

There's something about holidays that bring up and magnify our losses. We delight in gathering as families, but we're also keenly aware of those who are missing. Wonderful memories can bring forth both joy and sadness.

I think of feel-good holiday classics like *Miracle on 34th Street*, *It's a Wonderful Life*, and *White Christmas*. It's interesting that the backstories of these films include tragedy, illness, economic disaster, war, death, depression, and the difficulty of aging. Perhaps that's why they're classics. They give us hope. They're about overcoming our losses. Though life is tough, love and goodness can still win out.

Christmas Day 1977 was my first without dad. I've had many Christmases without him since. The ache has gotten better, but it's still there. I've gotten used to that hole in my heart and have learned to appreciate it. I miss him. I'm supposed to.

Grieving well is not about getting over your loved one. You don't get over a person. You learn to get through this time in the healthiest way possible. And that includes Thanksgiving, the Christmas holidays, and all the other special days of the year. Every one of them will remind you of your loss, and that's okay.

Like those holiday classic movies, many of your special days will be about overcoming. Your goal isn't to merely survive, but to make holidays work *for you* in less than ideal circumstances. With the right tools in your grief toolbox, you can create your own holiday classics, year after year.

Managing expectations, both your own and others', is a good life skill. It'll be especially important in the holidays following your loss. How can you begin to do that? We'll talk more about that as we go along.

Holidays can be tough. This year they might be extra hard, *but they can also be very good.*

THOUGHT QUESTIONS:

- What are your expectations of this holiday — for yourself, for your family, for others?

- What do you think others' expectations are?

- Which expectations create the most stress for you?

- Which expectations are simply unrealistic for the holidays this year?

Even with my loss,
this holiday can still be good.
I'll begin by managing my
own and others' expectations.

THIS HOLIDAY WILL BE DIFFERENT

"To be honest, I'm nervous. No, I'm scared.
It's like I'm frozen and can't move.
How am I going to face the
holidays without him?"
Tina, who lost her husband

ONE THING IS CERTAIN: YOUR holidays will be different from now on.

Your holidays will be different because your life has been altered forever. Someone very special to you is missing.

No matter what the holiday, you probably have powerful memories of your loved one associated with it. These wonderful (or sometimes painful) experiences of the past can be triggered in an instant. Potential reminders are everywhere:

- A familiar song,

- A certain food aroma,
- A walk in a familiar place,
- A special movie or show,
- Certain special holiday events,
- Being with good friends you both enjoyed,
- Holiday cards arrive, addressed to just you.

All these remind you of your times together. You can't get away from them. There's a trigger around every corner.

The memories flood in. Everywhere you look you see your loved one. You could swear you hear their voice. Perhaps you can almost feel their touch. Then reality crushes in upon you. They're gone.

Yes, holidays will be different now.

Let me assure you of a few things:

It's okay to be where you are in the grief process. It is what it is.

You may feel like a mess. That's not surprising. Your life has turned topsy-turvy. Grief is messy. Holidays are messy.

Maybe you're more easily irritated. Anger is a part of loss. How could you not be upset?

Perhaps you're sad or even depressed at times. That's natural. Are you supposed to be happy and thrilled right now?

You wonder if you're going crazy. No, you're just in a crazy situation. It feels like your soul has been ripped apart. Everything has changed.

You seem to be exhausted all the time. Grief exacts a heavy toll on your resources. It's mentally, emotionally, and physically draining.

You wish you could be stronger, but real strength lies in being real with your own heart. You're stronger than you know.

You're forgetting things right and left. Yep, that's part of grieving too.

So what do you need to do?

Be kind to yourself.
Give yourself more wiggle-room.
Don't expect as much from yourself (or from others, for that matter).
Work on accepting where you are right now.

You don't have to like where you're at currently. In fact, you may hate it. That's okay.

This time is not business-as-usual. Far from it. This is new, uncharted territory. Even if you've had other losses, this loss is different. Every loss is unique.

This holiday *will* be different.

I survived Thanksgiving and Christmas of 1977 without my dad. I survived his birthday earlier that year too. But I thought about him a lot.

The anniversary of his death was terribly hard. I went to the graveside and sat there for what seemed like hours. I thought of all the things I missed about him, and it was a long list. I told him I loved him and wished he was still here.

Not having him at my high school graduation was awful. All my friends were celebrating with their families, and I felt so alone. I couldn't get out of there fast enough. As I ran across the floor, my dad's business partner grabbed my arm. "He was so, so proud of you," he said. I broke down and wept. Several friends sought me out and surrounded me. My adoptive family came cheering around the corner, smothering me in handshakes and hugs. Graduation was painful, but it was also good.

I missed him at every swim meet (I was a competitive swimmer through college). I kept expecting to hear his whistle. After a race I always looked back and to the left — because that's where he always was.

I graduated from college. I got married. I graduated from Seminary. I moved to Japan, Hawaii, Washington and then back to Texas. I adopted three little girls from Colombia. There were more milestones along the way and many since then. And more losses as well.

Dad wasn't there for any of them. I missed him every time.

Yes, my heart still aches.

I'm betting your heart aches too. That ache honors your loved one. The grief you feel is part of saying "I love you" to the one you've lost.

Being kind to yourself and accepting where you are will be the key to navigating holidays in a healthy manner.

Yes, this holiday will be different, *but it can still be good.*

THOUGHT QUESTIONS:

- How do you think this holiday will be different because of your loss?

- What do you think you're going to miss most about your loved one this holiday?

- What are some ways you can be kind to yourself during this time?

*My holidays will be different,
but they can still be good.*

Do you feel like you need more grief
support?

We would like to help.
Visit www.garyroe.com and check out our
free resources.

3

"I FEEL SO ALONE SOMETIMES"

> "I'm alone. I'm not really, but that's
> sure the way it feels."
> *Bruce, who lost his wife*

S ANDRA LOVED THE HOLIDAYS. HER apartment was surrounded by lights and her front door resembled a huge Christmas present, complete with a big red bow. I could hear the holiday music playing inside, and when she opened the door the scent of cinnamon massaged my senses. Sandra's smile was as bright as her lights. She loved the holidays.

As I walked in, the first thing I noticed was her tree. It was absolutely beautiful — an eclectic blend of colorful ornaments spanning several generations. As I admired it, Sandra gave me the history of each ornament — who it was from, when, and the story behind it.

Then she guided me to the table, which

was covered with placemats made of old Christmas cards attached together and carefully laminated. Once again, she could tell me who sent each card and when.

As she shared these stories, Sandra went through a variety of emotions. She would smile, laugh, and cry. Sometimes she grew silent for a few moments. With almost every good and happy memory there was a companion story of loss.

As Sandra slipped into the kitchen to fix tea, I thought about all those memories. Her decorations had deep meaning for her. They represented her life — the ups, the downs, the trials, and the joys. Her life was all about people.

I turned and looked at her fireplace. Four stockings hung on the mantle. Sandra's was on the far left. The other three were for Sam (her recently departed husband), Steve (a son she lost in a car accident decades ago), and Ralph (a deceased brother).

I began to feel the weight of the losses Sandra had endured. I was surrounded by them everywhere I looked.

When Sandra came back in the room, she was no longer smiling. Her face was streaked with tears. She eased herself into the chair beside me and said, "This is so hard. I miss him so much. I miss them all so much. I feel so very alone now."

When you lose someone, your world comes to an abrupt halt. It's like everything is happening in slow motion. It feels surreal. People often describe it as *moving around in a fog*.

And the world doesn't seem to care. It goes right on spinning. People get up, go to work, watch ball games, and laugh like they don't have a care. Some people acknowledge your loss, but they also expect you to get past it quickly.

You sense that some people are uncomfortable around you. The truth is they're uncomfortable around grief and loss. It frightens them, or perhaps triggers significant losses they've experienced. In either case, that's about them and not about you, but it's tough just the same.

You might know others who've been

through similar losses. They're wonderful resources because they "get it." They know what you're going through — sort of. They can't understand fully because it's not their loss. It's yours. Your relationship with your loved one was unique — whether it was terrific, good, or difficult.

In the end, no one *really* understands. How can they? They're not you. *You* miss the one you lost. *You* miss their voice, their touch, their presence. Your loss is unique to *you*.

No wonder you feel alone.

The fact that you feel alone actually honors the memory of your loved one and your relationship with them. The intensity of your emotions shouts how important they were to you.

You've been hit and hit hard. The wound is deep and the pain is intense. And even as you heal, a large bruise begins to appear. Every time that bruise gets bumped, the pain flashes over you again. The size of the bruise corresponds to the importance of the relationship.

Holidays will bump your bruises. Pain and loneliness are natural results. In other words, feeling alone is okay. It's normal when you're grieving.

What do you do when the loneliness strikes? Just feel it. Acknowledge it. Try saying out loud, "I feel lonely."

Then try going further. "I feel lonely because I miss you. I miss..."

This gets your emotions out on the table. As you express them, they will often subside. The more you attempt to hide them, the more they will leak out in your life in other ways.

Your bruise is being bumped. You need to feel the pain.

It was Christmas 2002. Our family was celebrating my daughters' first Christmas in the United States. It was crazy — crazy wonderful. There was enough laughter in our family that day to fill a large arena.

However, at quieter times during the day a deep feeling of sadness would surface. Each time I shrugged it off. It wasn't until I got into bed that evening that I understood.

I missed my dad. He wasn't there for his granddaughters' first Christmas. I closed my eyes and could imagine him in the living room, holding them one by one in his lap, telling jokes, and having a glorious time.

I suddenly felt very alone.

Even after 25 years, the truth hit home again — *every* holiday is different now.

It's okay to feel alone, but watch out for the tendency to isolate. This affects some people more than others. When we're in pain, we naturally pull inward. If we're not careful, we can go internal and withdraw from relationships and activities.

Pulling back for a little while can be healthy. Deciding which activities and relationships you're going to invest in during this season of grief is very wise. Isolating yourself, however, is not a good idea. You need alone time *and* time with people. Healthy grieving involves a balance of both, depending on your personality and needs.

How do you find that balance? We'll talk more about that in the next chapter.

One other thing. You might feel alone, but I don't think you ever are. I believe there is One who is always there and who understands completely. He not only knows what you feel, *I believe he actually feels it with you.*

He journeys with you through the valley of grief. He will give you people who will walk with you as well. *You will get through this.*

THOUGHT QUESTIONS:

- When have you felt the most alone since your loss?

- How do you usually respond when you feel alone?

- How might you find a good balance between having the alone time you need but not isolating yourself?

I'll feel alone sometimes.
I need alone time, but I'll be careful
not to isolate myself.

4

YOUR HEART WILL BE THE KEY

"Above all else, guard your heart; it is the
wellspring of your life."
King Solomon

S AL AND MILDRED CALLED THEMSELVES *December people.* They were both born in December and were married on Christmas Eve. "We just partied all month long!" Mildred said.

When Mildred passed in early December, Sal wasn't surprised.

"She waited until our party month. Now she's having a party in heaven. I just wish I could be there," he said.

Sal looked down at his coffee and sighed. "I don't know how I'm going to make it through this month. I've got this pain under my heart. It hurts so much. What am I going to do?"

Sal was talking about emotional pain. His

heart had taken a serious hit and just the thought of the holiday season was overwhelming.

We talked about how to guard his heart and make the holidays work for him in the midst of his grief.

Your most prized possession is your heart. Without it you cannot be in relationship, give or receive love, or live with any kind of meaning or purpose. Your heart defines who you are. As King Solomon said, *your heart is the wellspring of your life.*

The world isn't easy on hearts. Pain and disappointment hammer us. Disaster and tragedy seem to strike randomly. Negativity swirls around us like a cloud of gnats. Anxiety and anger surface and grow.

Then we get socked with a devastating loss. Our hearts tremble.

These things threaten to silence our hearts. We can't let that happen.

Take King Solomon's advice: you must guard your heart.

How do you do that?

1. **Take your heart seriously**.

   You're grieving. Grief takes immense energy. Your heart needs time to recover. This isn't a sprint, but a marathon. You're going to have to pace yourself.

   "Grieving is the hardest work I've ever done. It's like I got hit by a truck. Did I walk away unscathed? No. I'll be recovering for a long time — and need a lot of help from others along the way." – *Samantha, who lost her husband*

   You've been hit by a truck. *You must take your heart seriously.*

2. **Protect your heart from danger**.

   Here are three things to watch out for this holiday season:

   The Busy-ness Trap
   Holidays are busy, especially the time from Thanksgiving to Christmas. Go, go, go! Do, do, do! There are family activities, special events, civic celebrations, and church services. We plan, prepare, and go shopping in the middle of the night.

'Tis the season to be stressed out, fa-la-la-la-la, la-la-la-la...

It's a trap. Don't get snared by it.

"The best thing I did this holiday season was to *slow down*. It was tough, but I'm so glad I did. Life was hard enough as it was without exhausting myself even further." – *Kris, who lost her mother*

Under normal circumstances, holidays are incredibly challenging. You're trying to adjust to a new normal, and you need breathing room. Too much activity squeezes your heart and hinders healthy grieving.

The Expectation Treadmill

We talked about expectations in the first chapter. Everybody has them. This holiday can't be about pleasing others and making people happy. People-pleasing is like a treadmill. Once you step on, it's hard to get off. The longer you stay on, the faster the treadmill goes. You just end up exhausting yourself while going nowhere.

"People were disappointed when I didn't do some of the usual things this year. They wanted things to be the same, but things aren't the same. I'd have been faking it." – *Steve, who lost his daughter*

It's not your job to make people happy. You can't. They have to make that choice for themselves.

Don't get on the expectation treadmill. You can make these holidays work for you.

The Santa Syndrome

Who doesn't want to play Santa Clause? But *Ho-ho-ho* isn't exactly where you're at right now. You may be tempted to hide your grief in an attempt to convince everyone (or yourself) that you're okay. You think that perhaps if you give, give, give, you can escape the pain.

"I tried to run from the pain of her death. I wore a mask, trying to convince myself and others I was fine. I wasn't fine. Stuffing my grief led to some terrible decisions." – *John, who lost his wife*

You're not Santa, at least not right now. Guard your heart by giving yourself permission to grieve at Thanksgiving, Christmas, New Year's, anniversaries, and birthdays. We're healthier when we choose to live in reality.

Watch out for the Busy-ness Trap, the Expectation Treadmill, and the Santa Syndrome. Guard your heart and don't get sucked into attitudes and activities that are not healthy for you right now.

3. **Be proactive in your choices.**

People who don't do what's good for them in times of grief usually end up resenting it (and the people involved) later. You can't afford to let the holidays control you. You have a choice about where to go, what to be involved in, and with whom.

"I can't control everything, but I do have control over some things. I'm trying to focus on using what I can control to help me grieve well." – *Clark, who lost his son*

You have choices. You can make wise ones that help you and those around you honor your loved one and grieve well. We'll talk more about this in the next chapter.

Take time with your own heart. Get in touch with what's going on inside. Acknowledge what you're feeling. Be nice to yourself.

Guard your heart. Nurture it. It is the well from which everything else flows.

THOUGHT QUESTIONS:

- What would it look like for you to take your heart seriously this holiday?

- Which danger are you most likely to fall into: the Busy-ness Trap, the Expectation Treadmill, or the Santa Syndrome? What can you do about that?

- What's out of your control this holiday? What can you control? Do you believe you can make proactive choices and do this holiday well?

If I want to do the holidays well, I must pay attention to my heart.

5

HOW TO MAKE WISE CHOICES

"This holiday is important. I want
to do this right."
Nancy, who lost her sister

ON SUNDAY AFTERNOON DURING THE holidays,
I ran into Chris and Karen in the grocery
store. The moment I laid eyes on them, I knew
something was wrong. They seemed to be
moving in slow motion, shuffling their feet
and staring blankly ahead. I was almost on
top of them before they noticed me. They
looked exhausted.

"Hey guys. Are you okay?" I asked.

They looked at one another, and then Chris
said, "Actually, no. When Karen's mom passed
away, we knew the holidays were going to be
hard, but we never dreamed they would be
like this."

"I've never been so tired and frustrated

in my life. I feel like such a failure," Karen added, and began to cry.

We maneuvered to a little café area where Chris and Karen told me their story. Their kids had a tough time with grandma not being there. Grandpa seemed withdrawn, hopeless and lost since she passed. Karen tried to be strong and make Christmas more special than it had ever been before. She and Chris purchased more presents than usual and planned an abundance of family activities. Their calendar was packed.

When Christmas rolled around, nobody talked about grandma, but you could tell she was on their minds. They tried to laugh and to celebrate, but a cold, sad silence would frequently descend upon them.

And with each passing day, Chris and Karen got more fatigued. Everyone became irritable. The kids seemed to be angry at everything and everyone. Karen's dad would sit and stare at the walls or wander off. Nobody was having any fun, so Karen and Chris tried even harder.

Now here they were, weeping in a grocery store café.

Chris and Karen's story is not unusual.

They were exhausted before the holidays hit, and they just kept pushing.

Grief is terribly draining. You're going to be tired. You're going to need more rest than usual. Just the routine activities of life will seem overwhelming at times.

That's because your gas tank is empty. You're running on fumes.

I often say that my middle daughter is living proof that God exists. After she got her driver's license, she managed to run out of gas four times in one year — each time right smack in front of our house.

"How do you do it?" I asked her.

"I don't know daddy. Just lucky I guess," she answered with a grin.

"And how do you manage to run out of gas in the first place?"

"I guess I just don't pay attention," she responded.

There's some very simple wisdom tucked away in that story: *If we don't pay attention to how much is in our tank, we'll likely run out of gas.*

Your tank is not full. It can't be. Chances are it's near empty. You're grieving. Good and healthy grieving takes a lot of energy, and when you're sad, hurt, or angry, it's difficult to want to do the things that put gas back in your tank.

When you have a limited supply of gas in the tank and no viable opportunity to fill up any time soon, what do you do?

Limit how much you drive. Drive in a cost-efficient, wise manner. And keep a close eye on the gas tank.

What does that mean for the holidays?

Be wise.
Make good choices.
You're most likely going to have to do less.

Knowing why you do what you do on holidays is important. Usually, holiday activities fit into one of the following categories:

"It's tradition."

Traditions are rituals handed down across generations that have meaning for you and other family members. These activities are part of your family identity.

Most likely some if not all your holiday traditions involved your loved one somehow. You have to decide whether you want to continue that tradition this year, and if so, how. Maybe someone else could head up that tradition this year.

One of the best ways I've found to go at this is for you to not make that decision alone. Include family members in the process.

What do they want to do with that tradition this year?

What seems most consistent with the situation and where family members are in their grief?

What would honor your loved one the most?

As you discuss this as a family, usually things will come to resolution pretty quickly. And most importantly, you've talked about the huge elephant in the room — your departed loved one and how you're going to celebrate this holiday without them.

Good things come out of healthy communication about this as a family.

"I have to!"

It's amazing how much of our holidays revolve around what we sense we *have* to do — our obligations.

What are your typical holiday obligations? Do you really *have* to do that this year? If it has to be done, do *you* have to do it?

You're running on much less than a full tank. Obligations use gas that might be needed for things of higher priority.

"That's just the way I do it!"

Some holiday activities are *habits*. We've always done them, or done them in a certain way. Unlike traditions, habits have little to no intrinsic meaning to them. They're just our routine.

Routine is important, however, especially in times of emotional distress or upheaval. Habits give us a sense of control, which is comforting when we're journeying through unfamiliar territory.

Which of your holiday activities fall into the habit category?

Do you want to keep that habit this year?
Is that habit comforting to you, or is it time
to make a change?

"I want to."

I-want-to stuff is the most fun of all. It falls into the just-because category, and doesn't need to make sense to anyone else.

And yes, the I-want-to stuff might also be a tradition, a habit, or even an obligation. The key is *you want to.*

What do you want to do this holiday?
Where do you want to go?
Whom do you want to go with?

Again, the key words are *want-to.*

Remember, if you're at a quarter-of-a-tank right now, there's only so much you can do. Guard you heart. Make wise choices. You'll be glad you did.

THOUGHT QUESTIONS:

- Make a list of your typical holiday activities. Label them according to whether they are traditions, obligations, habits, or want-tos. Does anything strike you about your list?

- How are you going to handle traditions this holiday? Be sure to try and include family members in this process (this will help manage everyone's expectations).

- What do you want to do this holiday and with whom? How can you make sure that happens?

*I will watch my gas tank carefully.
This holiday I will choose what I'm going to
do, when, and with whom.*

Grief is lonely, but the grief road is well
populated.

Consider becoming a part of our free
Caring for Grieving Hearts Community on
Facebook.
https://www.facebook.com/garyroeauthor

6

SAFE PEOPLE CAN KEEP YOU SANE

"I can't believe what some people will say.
How can they be so insensitive?"
Melanie, who lost her husband

STEPHANIE LOOKED SHOCKED.
"I'm so angry," she said. "I just had lunch with a friend. It was my mom's favorite restaurant, so I knew it was going to be tough. I cried when they brought out the salad. And do you know what my friend said? 'Are you still sad? When are you going to get over this?'"

"Seriously?! My mom's only been gone six weeks!" she continued.

Well-meaning people can say the dumbest things.

"You just have to be strong."

"It's okay. Don't cry!"

"Don't be sad. You should be thankful for all the memories."

"Come on and snap out of this. Get over it."

Perhaps people who say these things have never had a significant loss or been struck by the lightning bolt of grief. In most cases, they're simply uncomfortable with pain and displays of emotion. They don't know what to do and feel out of control. So they try to fix it, make you feel better, or shut you up. They usually end up making it worse.

I would not describe Stephanie's friend as a safe person. She judged Stephanie and invalidated her feelings. It's as if she said, "Your mom didn't really matter that much. What's wrong with you?"

Everyone needs safe people in their life.

A safe person:

- Meets you where you are and accepts you as you are, feelings and all,

- Listens well and is genuinely interested in you,
- Doesn't evaluate, judge, or try to fix,
- Doesn't give advice unless asked,
- Doesn't try to help you feel better,
- Has no plans for your improvement,
- Is honored to walk with you through your valley.

You need a safe person. He or she might be a good friend or a relative, but maybe not. They could be an acquaintance, a pastor, someone from a Care Ministry Team at church, or a professional counselor.

You need at least one safe person, but several would be nice.

Safe people don't grow on trees. Many people don't have the tools to be safe. Because of deficits in their own lives, many feel compelled to fix or control. These folks typically don't respond well to grief. *It might be wise to limit your exposure to them during this time.*

When someone does say something insensitive, consider giving them one of the following canned responses:

- *"Thanks for your concern."*
- *"It's tough. Thanks for your support."*
- *"I'm working on it."*
- *"I'm taking my time. I want to do this well."*

The best response might be no response at all. Perhaps just look them in the eye and smile. That leaves the ball in their court where it belongs. They need to deal with their own emotions about your grief.

Thankfully, I have a number of safe people in my life. I don't see them on a daily basis, but I try to touch base with at least one every day, even if it's just an email, text, phone call, or Facebook. Even a very brief connection with them can help settle my heart.

The members of my adoptive family that took me in after my dad died are powerfully safe people. When I'm with any of them, especially the parents, my heart immediately begins to relax. It's as if nothing bad could happen, and even if it did, everything would somehow be okay.

I have five other friends with whom I can talk about anything, share any emotion, and know they'll be with me in it. They're safe people who keep me grounded, focused, and sane.

Who are the safe people in your life?

If you don't have a friend or relative you would call safe, do you know someone else who might be?

"When my friend Kirk walks in the room, peace comes with him," David said. "I can be myself. I'm not fine, and I can act not-fine with him. He takes whatever I throw at him."

"When I lost Meg, I thought my life was over," he continued. "Because of Kirk, I'm beginning to think I just might survive this. And you know what? Yesterday, I met a guy at the hardware store who lost his wife last week. We went out for coffee, and I just listened. I knew exactly where he was coming from. We're going to get together again soon. Maybe I can be a Kirk for him."

Safe people tend to rub off on you. Not only do you feel safe around them, but after a while you begin to carry their safety away with you. You become a little more like them. As you walk through your grief in a healthy way, you'll find yourself becoming a safe person for others. You'll discover new tools and fill your toolbox. Those tools won't be just for you, but also for others you meet down the road.

That means your loss isn't just about you and your loved one. It's far bigger. As you heal, you become someone who can help others heal. If you focus on traveling your own dark valley well, you'll become an experienced valley-walker who can love others in the midst of their pain.

Grief can give us good gifts. We receive these when we accept things as they are — including our loss and all the emotions, concerns, and fears that accompany it. When we accept ourselves in this process, over time we quit fighting the emotions and begin to relax. Our new normal begins to take shape. Our loss takes its proper place as we move forward, and the color slowly begins to seep back into life.

Safe people help immensely in this journey. They're like rest-stops along the grief super-highway — places our souls can relax and be comforted.

I believe God provides safe people to walk

with us through the valley of sorrow and grief. We just have to recognize them.

Safe people accept you as you are.
Safe people don't try to fix you or help you feel better.
Safe people are genuinely interested in you and listen well.
Safe people are honored that you trust them with your pain and grief.
Safe people can keep you sane and grounded.

Find a safe person. Get together with them. Share with them how you're doing, and watch what happens.

THOUGHT QUESTIONS:

- Who are the safe people in your life? If you don't know any, how might you find one?

- Do you spend time regularly with at least one safe person? If not, how can you schedule time with them this week?

- How might you respond to a well-meaning person who says something dumb? It's great to have a couple of canned responses ready to go when you need them.

Safe people will help me stay grounded and sane.
I will find and treasure them.

7

THIS HOLIDAY WITH YOUR LOVED ONE

"People tell me I need to move on. No thanks. I can't leave her behind."
Jeremy, who lost his daughter

"PEOPLE KEEP TELLING ME I have to move on, but I don't want to!" Kelly yelled through her tears. "It feels like moving on means leaving Connor behind. I can't. I just can't."

"In fact, I won't!" she said.

Kelly had lost her son Connor in an accident six months previously. She had been dreading the holidays, but was doing the best she could for the sake of her other three kids.

"Who said you have to leave Connor behind? You can't. That's impossible. He's part of you. You take him with you wherever you go," I said.

Kelly turned and stared at me. She gazed into my eyes for a long moment and then asked, "Could you say that again?"

I repeated myself, and then added, "When someone dies, *we don't move on without them. We move on with them, but in a new way.*"

"Move on with Connor in a new way," she whispered. "I just have to figure out what that is."

"That's right. What do you think that might mean?" I asked.

For the next half-hour, Kelly talked about how she could honor Connor with her grief and express her love for him by keeping his memory alive. She considered how she could let him take his new place in their family — physically absent, but yet a part of them always.

Then she made specific, proactive plans for the holidays.

Yes, your loved one is gone. They're no longer physically present with you, but think of all the profound influence they've had in your life. They've impacted you deeply and permanently. They helped make you who you are.

Though you may not always be aware of it, they're a part of you and always will be. Nothing can ever take that from you.

So your task this holiday is not to move on without them, but move on with them in a new way.

Use this holiday to honor them and your relationship in a good and healthy way.

Here's what others have done for the Thanksgiving and Christmas holidays:

"He always sat at the head of the table. We left an *empty chair* there. After Thanksgiving dinner, we stayed at the table and shared what we remembered and missed most about him. It was emotional, but so good and so healing." – *Penny, who lost her husband*

"We put *a stocking* up for her every year. All of us, including the kids, write a letter or card to her and put it in the stocking along with any special little things we want to give her. We read those letters out loud on Christmas morning. Everyone looks forward to it. It's really helped us heal." – *Connie, who lost her daughter*

"She loved Christmas decorations, so I went out and bought *a tree ornament that reminded me of her*. I put it on the family tree that year and told everyone why. It set off a chain reaction of sharing. I think I'll be able to smile at Christmas now." – *Frank, who lost his wife*

"Our family talked together about what we wanted to do to honor grandpa during the holidays. We decided to *volunteer at the homeless mission*. We knew grandpa would be proud of that. It was so good, and we talked and laughed about him the whole time. I think we've started a new tradition." – *Suzanne, who lost her father*

"Granny always ran to the door to greet visitors, so *we lit a candle* and put it in the entryway. Some family members even stopped and talked to the candle on their way in and out. It set just the right tone, like she was right here with us." – *Carl, who lost his mom*

"We had *a special night where we invited family and friends to come over and share memories*. We had a wonderful time. It set the stage for the whole holiday." – *Andy, who lost his brother*

"We got permission, *bought a tree and planted it* outside his old room at the nursing home. The whole family got involved, all the way down to the great grandkids. It was great." – *Lucy, who lost her dad*

As you figure out how to move on with your loved one in a new way, you'll find yourself creating new Christmas classics.

Thanksgiving and Christmas aren't the only challenging times you'll face. What about the other special days out there?

Here are a few more ideas:

"We decided to have a birthday party. We had a cake made that said, 'Happy First

Birthday in Heaven.' We put one candle on it. Before we sang Happy Birthday, we all shared at least one thing about Pop we were thankful for. There were lots of tears, but even more love and laughter." – *Jenny, who lost her father*

"We had a balloon release on her birthday. We gave everyone a balloon and a Sharpie. We all wrote a message to grandma on our balloons. Then we went outside and released them together." – *Doug, who lost his mother*

"With mom's permission, we had her wedding ring made into a pendant. We had a dinner on mom and dad's anniversary, and set an empty chair in dad's normal place. We gave her the pendant saying that even though dad was no longer with her, she carried him in heart. And of course, the pendant was on a chain long enough so that it rested right on her heart. It was an amazing evening." – *Craig, who lost his father*

"My friends couldn't stand the thought of me being alone on Valentine's Day, so they had a party. They didn't want me to feel awkward, so it was a ladies' only event. We had it early so they could still have time later with their guys. All the guys cooperated in this too. I felt so loved." – *Rebecca, who lost her husband*

The possibilities are endless.

What did your loved one enjoy? What reminds you of them? Is there a tradition that they were a major part of? Do you want to continue that or tweak it?

Remember, the elephant is already in the room. Bring it out into the open. Celebrate the life of your loved one. Yes, it might be tough. It will certainly be emotional, but it can be so good. Use your grief to help you heal.

Don't try to leave your loved one behind. That won't work. They're a part of you. Talk with your safe people, family, and friends about *how you can move on with your loved one in a new way*. Be proactive. You'll be so glad you did.

THOUGHT QUESTIONS:

- What did your loved one really enjoy? What sorts of things remind you of them?

- Based on your answers to the previous question, what can you do this holiday to honor them and your relationship with them?

- Is there a tradition that your loved one was a major part of? What does your family want to do with that? How can you tweak things so it helps everyone *move on with them*?

I don't have to leave my loved one behind. I can be creative and move on with them in new ways.

8

THE ULTIMATE GRIEF EXPERT

"Nothing is as comforting as the
presence of God."
Richard, who lost his wife

IT WAS THE DAY AFTER my dad died. I was
sitting with my best friend in the front room
of the apartment my dad and I had lived in.

The doorbell rang, and in walked my
friend's youth pastor.

I attended the same church but hadn't gone
to youth group because of school and athletic
obligations. Yet, here was the youth pastor in
my apartment.

I don't remember any of our conversation.
I don't recall anything he said. All I remember
is one particular phrase in his prayer: *"Lord,
you are the Alpha and the Omega."*

That phrase resonated in my heart. I heard

it over and over in the quieter moments of the next several months.

"Lord, you are the Alpha and the Omega."

I didn't know what to make of it at the time, but I somehow knew that God had spoken to me. He was with me. He knew. He understood. He cared.

"Lord, you are the Alpha and the Omega."

He knew it all. It might not make sense to me, but it did to him. At that moment, in the middle of that youth pastor's prayer, I knew my dad wasn't the only father I had.

Soon after I moved in with my new family, I was in Sunday worship with them and it was during the pastor's message. I was still in a daze and wasn't really listening.

All of a sudden it was like someone tapped me on the shoulder to get my attention. The next phrase out of the pastor's mouth made my heart skip a beat.

"A Father to the fatherless, a defender of widows, is God in his dwelling. God sets the lonely in families..." He was reading from Psalm 68.

I sat there in shock. Again, I knew God was speaking to me.

"A Father to the fatherless...God sets the lonely in families..."

My adoptive sister nudged me and smiled. I looked past her down the row. Every member of my new family was leaning forward, smiling at me. My new dad nodded.

I was overwhelmed.

God was going to take care of me. Though my dad's death came as a shock to me, it didn't take God by surprise. He knew all about it, and he had a plan for me.

I had lost my earthly biological dad, but I would always have a Father. And if I paid attention, he would always place other father-like figures in my life.

That was the promise I received that day in church. As I look back at the years from that day to this, he has been faithful. He has done what he promised.

This isn't surprising. God was just being God. Father to the fatherless, defender of the widows and provider of new families is just who he is. These things flow from his character. He loves.

He never promised my earthly dad would

always be here. God did promise that he would always be my Father.

Yes, Lord. You indeed are the Alpha and the Omega.

I could share many more examples, but let me get to the point. I am convinced, absolutely certain of the following things:

> *God loves you and will take care of you.*
> *He knows all about your loss and has a plan for your life now, after your loss.*
> *God wants to heal your heart and guide you as you grieve.*
> *God wants to comfort you and be intimately involved in your life.*

As you accept them, you'll find these truths sinking deeper into your heart. Eventually, you'll experience them in very personal ways.

John chapter 11 is a striking narrative about the death of the one of Jesus' closest friends — a man named Lazarus. Knowing that Lazarus had died, Jesus and his disciples made their way to the town of Bethany, where Lazarus resided with his two sisters, Mary and Martha.

As Jesus approached town, Martha ran out to meet him. She fell at his feet and said, "Lord, if you had been here, my brother would not have died."

Martha's family knew Jesus well. They had sent him a message that Lazarus was ill. Jesus had decided he would wait a few days before going to Bethany. Why? *Because his plan was to raise Lazarus from the dead.*

No one else knew this. No one would have believed it if they had known. In her grief, Martha expressed her pain. Her statement is one of both faith and of confusion. She knows Jesus could have healed him, so why didn't he come when requested?

Martha didn't know, couldn't know, that Jesus had something bigger in mind.

Later in the passage, Mary also ran to meet Jesus outside of town. She too fell at his feet and uttered, "Lord, if you had been here, my brother would not have died."

The sisters had obviously talked about this. It was their way of saying, "Lord, where were you? Why? We don't understand!"

How did Jesus respond?

He *didn't* say, "Hey! I know what I'm doing here. How dare you question me?"

He *didn't* correct them and shout, "Quit being so upset! Calm down. Be strong."

He *didn't* confront them with, "Oh please! Get over it. Grow up! Where's your faith?"

Instead, he told them who he was.

"I am the resurrection and the life. Anyone who believes in me will live, even if he dies. And whoever lives and believes in me will never die. Do you believe this?"

And then something amazing happened. Jesus saw the sisters and the mourners wailing and grieving. He knew he was about the raise his friend from the dead. And what did he do?

Jesus wept.

Jesus wept? Why?

Jesus' tears weren't for Lazarus because he was about the raise him from the dead. I believe Jesus felt the intensity of the grief around him. He entered into the mourners' pain and felt it with them. I believe he does the same thing today.

He is not just with you. He enters into your grief and feels it with you.

Yes, he loves you that much. More than you can imagine.

The prophet Isaiah called him *the man of sorrows.* Jesus Christ knows all about pain, abuse, and physical suffering. He knows all about death. He has personally experienced these things. *He knows.* He gets it. He walks with you through your valley. He feels and experiences your loss and pain with you.

And after Jesus experienced death, he conquered it. Now death is the portal into fully experiencing the eternal life that those who trust in him already have.

If you find yourself angry with God, don't worry. He's not threatened by your emotions. He can handle it. In fact, he wants you to express your heart to him. He already knows anyway, and yes, he still loves you.

So go ahead. Let it out. Mary and Martha did. He listened to them, loved them, and wept with them. *He'll do the same for you.*

Earlier in this chapter I shared four key truths. They're so important that I'm going to repeat them again here. I encourage you to read them slowly and let them sink in.

God loves you and will take care of you.
He knows all about your loss and has a plan for your life now, after this loss.
God wants to heal your heart and guide you as you grieve.
God wants to comfort you and be intimately involved in your life.

He is the Ultimate Grief Expert. You won't find a better Valley-Walker anywhere.

Yes Lord, you are the Alpha and the Omega.

THOUGHT QUESTIONS:

- Have you sensed God speaking to you in your grief? If so, what have you heard him saying?

- Try reading John chapter 11. What do you think God wants you to take away from this passage?

- Of the four truths in the previous section, which one impacts you the most? Why?

God is with me in my grief.
He is my comfort and healing.

Have you found this book helpful?

Consider sharing it with others: https://
www.garyroe.com/surviving-the-holidays/

Together, we can make a big difference.

ADDITIONAL RESOURCES

BOOKS

COMFORT FOR GRIEVING HEARTS: HOPE AND ENCOURAGEMENT FOR TIMES OF LOSS

We look for comfort. We long for it. Grieving hearts need it to survive. Written with heartfelt compassion, this easy-to-read, warm, and practical book reads like a caring conversation with a friend and is destined to become a classic for those looking for hope and encouragement in times of loss. Composed of brief chapters, *Comfort for Grieving Hearts* is designed to be read one chapter per day, giving you bite-sized bits of comfort, encouragement, and healing over time. Available through Amazon and most major online retailers. For more information or to download a free excerpt, visit www.garyroe.com.

TEEN GRIEF: CARING FOR THE GRIEVING TEENAGE HEART

Teens are hurting. While trying to make sense of an increasingly confusing and troubled world, teens get hit, again and again. Edgy, fun-loving, tech-driven, and seemingly indestructible, their souls are shaking. We can't afford to allow pain and loss to get the better of them. Written at the request of parents, teachers, coaches, and school counselors, this informative, practical book is replete with guidance, insight, and ideas for assisting teens navigate the turbulent waters of loss. *Teen Grief* is a Winner of the 2018 Book Excellence Award and has received rave reviews from those who live and work with teens. *Teen Grief* is available in both paperback and electronic versions. For more information or to download a free excerpt, visit www.garyroe.com.

SHATTERED: SURVIVING THE LOSS OF A CHILD

Unthinkable. Unbelievable. Heartbreaking. Whatever words we choose, they all fall far short of the reality. The loss of a child is a terrible thing. How do we survive this?

Written at the request of grieving parents and grandparents, *Shattered* has been called "one of the most comprehensive and practical grief books available." The book combines personal stories, compassionate guidance, and practical suggestions/ exercises designed to help shattered hearts navigate this devastating loss. Honored as a 2017 Best Book Awards Finalist, *Shattered* became an Amazon #1 Bestseller soon after its publication and has received sterling reviews by both mental health professionals and grieving parents. It is available in both paperback and electronic versions on Amazon and most other major online book retailers. For more information or to download a free excerpt, visit www.garyroe.com.

PLEASE BE PATIENT, I'M GRIEVING: HOW TO CARE FOR AND SUPPORT THE GRIEVING HEART

People often feel misunderstood, judged, and even rejected during a time of loss. This makes matters more difficult for an already broken heart. It doesn't have to be this way. It's time we took the grieving heart seriously. Gary wrote this book by request to help others better understand and support grieving hearts, and to help grieving hearts understand themselves. A group discussion guide is included. *Please Be Patient, I'm Grieving* became a #1 Amazon Bestseller soon after its release and was honored as a 2016 Best Book Awards Finalist. It can be found in both paperback and electronic formats on Amazon and most other major online bookstores. For more information or to download a free excerpt, visit www.garyroe.com.

HEARTBROKEN: HEALING FROM THE LOSS OF A SPOUSE

Losing a spouse is painful, confusing, and often traumatic. This comforting and practical book was penned from the stories of dozens of widows and widowers. It's simple, straightforward approach has emotionally impacted hearts and helped thousands know they're not alone, not crazy, and that they will make it. An Amazon Top 10 Bestseller, *Heartbroken* was a 2015 USA Best Book Award Finalist and a National Indie Excellence Book Award Finalist. Available in paperback and electronic formats from Amazon and most major online retailers. For more information or to download a free excerpt, visit www.garyroe.com.

SAYING GOODBYE: FACING THE LOSS OF A LOVED ONE

Full of stories, this warm, easy-to-read, and beautifully illustrated gift book has comforted thousands. It reads like a conversation with a close friend, giving wise counsel and hope to those facing a loss. Co-authored with *New York Times' Bestseller* Cecil Murphey, this attractive hardback edition is available at www.garyroe.com/saying-goodbye.

FREE ON GARY'S WEBSITE

THE GOOD GRIEF MINI-COURSE

Full of personal stories, inspirational content, and practical assignments, this 8-session mini-course is designed to help readers understand grief and deal with its roller-coaster emotions. Several thousand have been through this course, which is now being used in support groups as well. Available at www.garyroe.com.

THE HOLE IN MY HEART: TACKLING GRIEF'S TOUGH QUESTIONS

This powerful e-book tackles some of grief's big questions: "How did this happen?"

"Why?" "Am I crazy?" "Am I normal?" "Will this get any easier?" plus others. Written in the first person, it engages and comforts the heart. Available at www.garyroe.com.

I MISS YOU: A HOLIDAY SURVIVAL KIT

Thousands have downloaded this brief, easy-to-read, and very personal e-book. *I Miss You* provides some basic, simple tools on how to use holiday and special times to grieve well and love those around you. Available at www.garyroe.com.

A REQUEST FROM THE AUTHOR

Thank you for taking your heart seriously and reading *Surviving the Holidays Without You*. I hope you found some comfort, healing, and practical help in its pages. I would love to hear what you thought of the book. Would you consider taking a moment and sending me a few sentences on how *Surviving the Holidays Without You* impacted you? Send me your thoughts at contact@garyroe.com. Your comments and feedback mean a lot to me and will assist me in producing more quality resources for grieving hearts. Thank you.

Warmly,
Gary

Visit Gary at www.garyroe.com and connect with him on Facebook, Twitter, LinkedIn, and Pinterest

Facebook: https://www.facebook.com/garyroeauthor

Twitter: https://twitter.com/GaryRoeAuthor

LinkedIn: https://www.linkedin.com/in/garyroeauthor

Pinterest: https://www.pinterest.com/garyroe79/

AFFIRMATIONS FOR HOLIDAYS

Try reading these affirmations repeatedly during holiday seasons. Reminding yourself of these truths can make a huge difference.

1. Even with my loss, this holiday can still be good. I'll begin by managing my own and others' expectations.
2. My holidays will be different, but they can still be good.
3. I'll feel alone sometimes. I need alone time, but I'll be careful not to isolate myself.
4. If I want to do the holidays well, I must pay attention to my heart.
5. I will watch my gas tank carefully. This holiday I will choose what I'm going to do, when, and with whom.

6. Safe people will help me stay grounded and sane. I will find and treasure them.

7. I don't have to leave my loved one behind. I can be creative and move on with them in new ways.

8. God is with me in my grief. He is my comfort and healing.

ABOUT THE AUTHOR

Gary's story began with a childhood of mixed messages and sexual abuse. This was followed by other losses and numerous grief experiences.

Ultimately, a painful past led Gary into a life of helping wounded people heal and grow. A former college minister, missionary in Japan, entrepreneur in Hawaii, and pastor in Texas and Washington, he now serves as a writer, speaker, chaplain, and grief counselor.

In addition to *Surviving the Holidays Without You*, Gary is the author of numerous books, including the award-winning bestsellers

Shattered: Surviving the Loss of a Child, Please Be Patient, I'm Grieving, and *Heartbroken: Healing from the Loss of a Spouse.* He has been featured on Focus on the Family, Dr. Laura, Beliefnet, the Christian Broadcasting Network, and other major media and has well over 500 grief-related articles in print. Recipient of the Diane Duncam Award for Excellence in Hospice Care, Gary is a popular keynote, conference, and seminar speaker at a wide variety of venues.

Gary loves being a husband and father. He has seven adopted children, including three daughters from Colombia. He enjoys hockey, corny jokes, good puns, and colorful Hawaiian shirts. Gary and his wife Jen and family live in Texas.

Visit Gary at www.garyroe.com.

Don't forget to download your free, printable PDF:
8 Tips for Handling Holiday Grief
https://www.garyroe.com/holiday-grief/
(for paperback version)

AN URGENT PLEA

HELP OTHER GRIEVING HEARTS

Dear Reader,

Others are hurting and grieving today. You can help.

How?

With a simple, heartfelt review.

Could you take a few moments and write a 1-3 sentence review of *Surviving the Holidays Without You* and leave it on Amazon?

Just go find Surviving the Holidays Without You on Amazon and then click on "Customer Reviews" just under the title.

And if you want to help even more, you could leave the same review on the *Surviving the Holidays Without You* book page on Goodreads.

Your review counts and will help reach others who could benefit from this book. Thanks for considering this. I read these reviews as well, and your comments and feedback assist me in producing more quality resources for grieving hearts.

Thank you!
Warmly,
Gary